THE TEACHERS MARCH!

Sandra Neil Wallace
and Rich Wallace

Illustrated by
Charly Palmer

How Selma's Teachers
Changed History

CALKINS CREEK
AN IMPRINT OF
BOYD MILLS & KANE
New York

Reverend F. D. Reese taught science at R. B. Hudson High School, but his favorite subject was freedom. He believed that everyone was a first-class citizen, just like the Constitution stated. To be treated as less than equal, that just wasn't right.

With fire in his eyes, Reverend Reese led marchers to the courthouse to register to vote.

Troublemakers. That's what the police called the marchers. Reverend Reese knew that was a lie. The marchers just wanted to vote like everybody else. But in Selma, Alabama, segregation kept black people and white people apart, and billy clubs kept black people from voting.

Sheriff Clark's cheeks boiled red whenever he spotted Reverend Reese and the marchers. His deputies blocked the marble steps of the courthouse. The sheriff swung his club at the reverend like he was a baseball, and that kept most people away.

Even if they made it into the courthouse, the reverend knew what would happen. *You must take a voting test!* A test impossible to pass. *How many drops of water are in the Alabama River?* How could anyone answer a question like that?

Reverend Reese pulled his trench coat over his bruises and kept on marching and talking about freedom. He had to find a way to make their voices heard. He needed a "triumphant idea."

Walking through the school one day, the reverend found his idea in every classroom. *What if the teachers marched?* Not just one teacher like him, but hundreds of teachers.

Leaders. That's what people called the teachers. The teachers were the *somebody* somebodies of the community. College educated. Shiny leather shoes. Suits and Sunday brooches seven days a week. No group like that had marched for freedom before.

If the teachers marched, people would notice, and change would come.

But in that summer of 1964, a judge declared marching and talking about voting rights against the law in Selma.

"Don't get involved in that mess," some people warned. "It's too dangerous." And that stopped meetings and marches to the courthouse.

How would Reverend Reese convince the teachers to march now? He searched for a "glorious opportunity."

Just before Christmas, he huddled by the TV, watching the great civil rights leader Dr. Martin Luther King Jr. talk about freedom. The reverend's face lit up like a Christmas tree. Who better than Dr. King to turn things around and help convince the teachers to march? That night, Reverend Reese wrote a letter to Dr. King, inviting him to Selma. He signed it, *Yours for Better Citizens*.

Some people thought, *There's no way Dr. King will come to Selma*. But Dr. King said yes!

Some preachers feared they'd be arrested if Dr. King spoke in their churches about voting rights. But not the pastor of Brown Chapel. He gave Reverend Reese permission to have Dr. King speak at his church.

When the day arrived, clouds hung so heavy they covered the steeples of Brown Chapel.

Reverend Reese worried that nobody would show up. The night before, a soldier home on leave for Christmas had thrown a smoke bomb near the church, hoping to scare Dr. King away.

The bomb didn't scare anyone away. Seven hundred people squeezed into Brown Chapel, waiting for Dr. King.

Fifteen-year-old Joyce Parrish sat in her usual row with her mother, "Too Sweet."

When Dr. King swung through the doors of Brown Chapel, Joyce and Too Sweet leapt to their feet and clapped. Dr. King said people shouldn't be afraid of being arrested. They should go to jail by the thousands to defend the right to vote. And he wasn't just talking about *committed* marchers like Reverend Reese. He meant *everybody* in Brown Chapel.

At the next meeting, Reverend Reese spoke to the teachers filling the church pews. He told them about his "triumphant idea."

"We're not just teachers in the classroom, but leaders in the community," he proclaimed. "People are looking to us to give leadership. We are going to march!"

The teachers fidgeted, as if they hadn't heard. Some sat still as statues. When times got this quiet, Reverend Reese always said, "You could hear a rat walk on cotton."

"I'll believe it when I see it," grumbled a churchgoer.

Teachers may be the *somebody* somebodies. And they taught school to thousands of kids. But when it came to marching? *They didn't have the courage.* That's what people whispered.

Reverend Reese noticed that the teachers were afraid. He knew what they were thinking: *If we march, we could get arrested. We could go to jail. We could lose our jobs!* Teachers had to be "sensible." The white superintendent of schools hired them because they had the "good sense" *not* to march.

But if the teachers didn't march, nothing would change.

The reverend needed a guarantee from the teachers. *Fast.* He waved a sheet of paper in the air. "If you will participate in a Teachers' March, sign this list," he urged. "Show up and show out!"

Reverend Reese explained that if both parents taught school, then only one would march. That way, somebody could take care of the kids if the other parent went to jail.

So where did that leave Too Sweet? She taught school, but she was also a mother—the only parent. Period. There was Joyce's grandmother, who cooked the food. But Too Sweet earned the money for it.

The first teacher to sign the list was Coach Lawrence Huggins. He was tired of telling kids about the Constitution—"freedom and justice for all!"— but not defending it for himself.

Another teacher signed up, and another, until more than a hundred teachers had pledged to march!

Before the meeting was over, Too Sweet stood up. She signed her name to the list.

The march was set for January 22. When Joyce woke up that morning, her mother kept busy in the kitchen. Without saying a word, Too Sweet put a peanut butter sandwich and a toothbrush in a brown paper bag. She'd need those things in jail.

The teachers had promised Reverend Reese they'd march to the courthouse that afternoon. But Joyce grew worried. Would Too Sweet be coming home that night? Joyce grabbed her mother and held her tight.

Later that day, Reverend Reese waited by the steps of the school with his list of names. Classes had ended, but the teachers weren't lined up. Had they changed their minds? Had they decided not to march?

Reverend Reese wouldn't blame them if they had. All week, he'd seen people getting arrested for trying to register to vote. Sheriff Clark herded them into an alley blocked with rope, like they were cattle. He locked them in jail. Even Dr. King was beaten and bruised. If that could happen to a *somebody* like Dr. King, would the teachers be brave enough to march?

The wind rustled Reverend Reese's list of names, but he kept his eyes on the school doors. He had faith in the teachers. They'd given him their word. They'd signed the list. But he was standing alone.

Suddenly, the doors burst open. One teacher walked out, then another.
They held toothbrushes in the air, ready to go to jail for freedom.
Soon, one hundred and four teachers strutted down the steps, their
toothbrushes gleaming like swords in the Selma sun.
"The teachers are gonna march!" kids shouted,
rousing people from the neighborhood.

Reverend Reese called Coach Huggins to
the front of the line. Coach was strong and
fearless. He taught weightlifting to the
football team and was in great shape.
Reverend Reese wanted him close by,
in case there was trouble.
Whenever anyone
marched, there was bound
to be trouble.

"Could you believe it?" grown-ups murmured, rushing from their homes. "The teachers are gonna march!"

Reverend Reese told the kids to wait at Brown Chapel, but Joyce paced nervously along the sidewalk, searching for Too Sweet. Would her mother be safe? If Too Sweet went to jail, they'd be anything but free. If Too Sweet got fired from her job, they'd be asking for handouts: food, clothing, *everything*.

"We are going to keep walking until we have reached the courthouse," Reverend Reese reminded the teachers.

Two by two, they started marching. The reverend walked in front, his hands clenched in his trench coat pockets. Coach Huggins, tall and strong. Too Sweet, poised and defiant. Teachers young and old, clutching paper bags filled with sandwiches for jail.

The teachers didn't breathe a word. They didn't smile or sing freedom songs. But you could hear the courage in their leather shoes churning up the red dirt road and see the bravery behind their Sunday brooches, catching the light of the sun.

When the teachers reached the white section of town, red dirt changed to pavement. Crowds gathered like storm clouds. Shopkeepers hurried out of their stores. They glared at the teachers, trying to rattle their courage.

"What is it that they want?" they wondered.

The teachers kept marching.

What they wanted was what everyone had: the right to vote.

As they turned onto Alabama Avenue, the teachers spotted the thirteen steps of green marble leading up to the courthouse.

Sheriff Clark and his deputies stood at the top of those steps.

When the sheriff saw so many teachers marching toward him, his eyes filled with rage.

"We are here to register," Reverend Reese announced.

"You can't make a plaything out of the corridors of this courthouse," the sheriff boomed. "You think you can make it a Disneyland."

"We have a right to be here," the reverend insisted.

"I will give you one minute to clear the steps," Clark roared, "or I'll have you all arrested."

The teachers folded their arms. Some gripped their paper bags tighter. But they refused to move.

"Ten seconds!" yelled the sheriff.

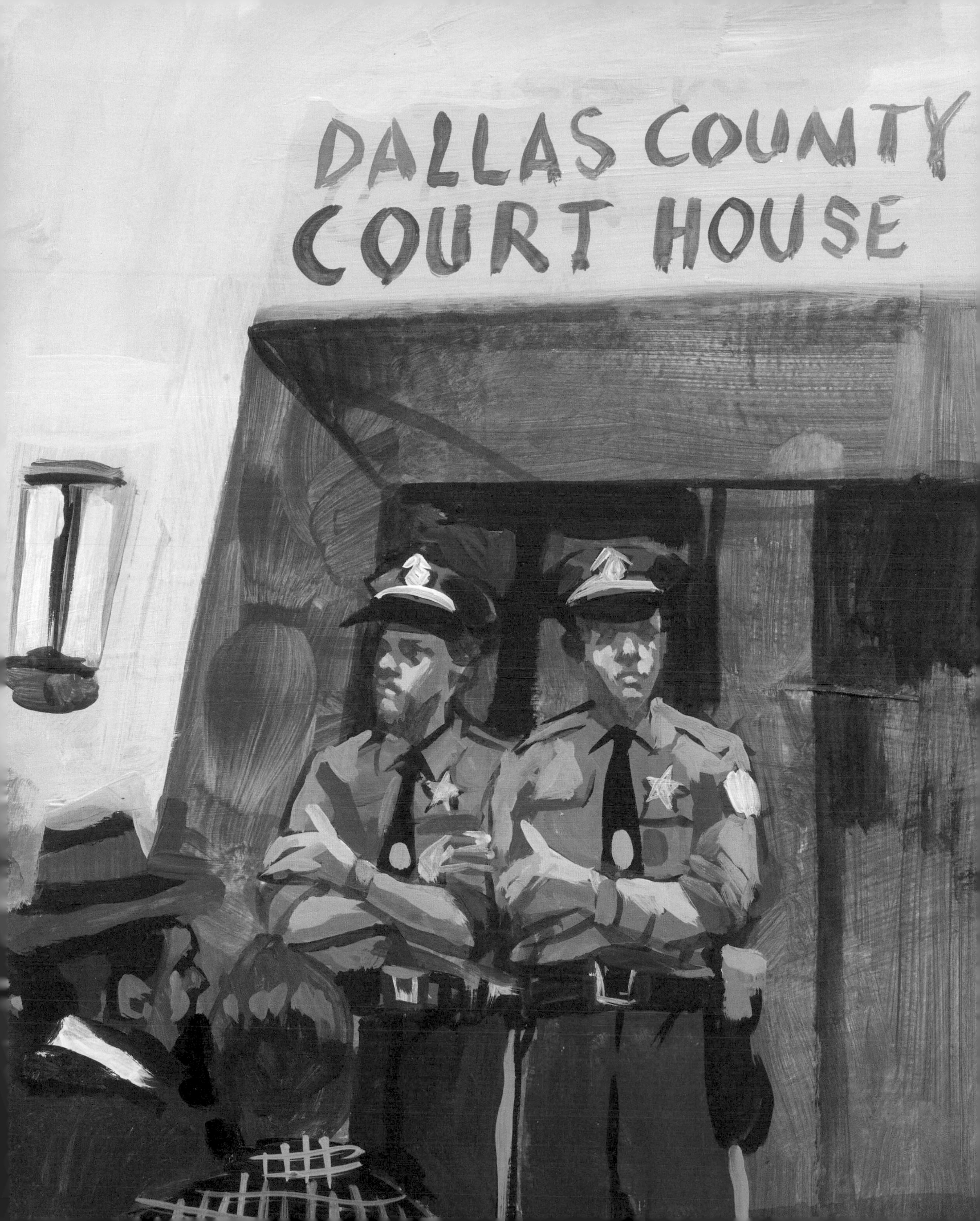
DALLAS COUNTY
COURT HOUSE

Reverend Reese and the teachers stood on the courthouse steps, as still as the Statue of Liberty.

"Time's up. Now move it!" Sheriff Clark and his deputies reached for their billy clubs. The sheriff jabbed Coach Huggins in the stomach, then Reverend Reese. The teachers fell down the steps like dominoes.

Reverend Reese led the teachers back up again.

Sheriff Clark grew so angry that he shoved the teachers down the steps even harder the second time.

The school superintendent rushed out of the courthouse. He stared at the teachers. He could fire each and every one of them—Reverend Reese, Coach Huggins, Too Sweet.

The teachers stared right back at him. They looked into the angry eyes of Sheriff Clark.

Go ahead, Reverend Reese kept thinking. *Arrest us.* This wasn't Disneyland. This was real life. First-class citizens. That's what they were. Nothing less. The Constitution guaranteed it. They'd stepped out for their right to vote, ready to be handcuffed—ready to lose their jobs for that right.

But if the superintendent fired every teacher lined up at the courthouse, who would teach the students? He would have to shut down the schools. Then he would be out of a job.

Reverend Reese knew it. So did Sheriff Clark.

The sheriff put away his billy club. The handcuffs stayed clasped to his waist.

Reverend Reese and his triumphant idea had gained a glorious victory.

Although the teachers didn't register to vote that day, the sheriff had the good sense not to arrest them, and the superintendent had the good sense not to fire them. With their heads held high, the teachers walked proudly to Brown Chapel.

The church thundered with the sounds of young voices singing freedom songs. "The teachers are coming back!" somebody shouted. Everyone stood and sang louder.

Joyce couldn't see the teachers, but she cheered anyway—
for Reverend Reese, for Coach Huggins, for Too Sweet. Too
Sweet *had* to be there.

"Did you see my teacher marching?" kids gushed across
wooden pews. As soon as the singing stopped, Joyce spun
around, searching for Too Sweet. When she found her, Joyce
ran and hugged her mother and wouldn't let go.

When Dr. King came back to preach that night, he praised Reverend Reese and the teachers for making civil rights history. No group of leaders had risked their jobs before by marching.

"We were like giants," Reverend Reese said with a smile. "Great giants!"

Because Reverend Reese and the teachers marched,
other groups started marching for their right to vote.
Beauticians and barbers marched. Then the undertakers
marched.

Because Reverend Reese and the teachers marched,
they became heroes to their students. It didn't matter that
the kids were too young to vote. They intended to march
for their teachers' and their parents' right to vote.

The students left school after roll call, when the teachers turned their backs to gaze out the window. "I'm gonna get you your civil rights," they promised their new heroes. They marched to the courthouse with determination in their eyes, and ankle socks and sneakers on their feet. Joyce marched too, for her mother, Too Sweet.

The Selma marchers filled the jails by the thousands.

Americans noticed. They wondered why respectable citizens in suits and dresses, and school kids carrying books, were jailed.

The president of the United States noticed. He pushed for a new voting rights law.

That summer of 1965, the Voting Rights Act passed. It made certain that nobody had to take a test just to vote.

On one August morning, Reverend Reese, Too Sweet, and the other teachers walked down Alabama Avenue. They climbed the steps of the federal building across from the courthouse.

Inside, there were no voting tests, no billy clubs, no alleys marked with rope. All the teachers had to do was sign their names and they were registered to vote.

The first thing they did was vote Sheriff Clark out of office.

AUTHORS' NOTE

Reverend F. D. Reese and Joyce Parrish O'Neal

The Selma Teachers' March was a major turning point in the civil rights movement. In 1965, Dr. Martin Luther King Jr. said that the march was the first time such a well-organized and dramatic protest had been made by a group of black professionals.

Yet few have ever heard of the Teachers' March or the people responsible for leading it. We found out about the march while interviewing several foot soldiers of the Selma voting rights movement for our biography about activist Jonathan Myrick Daniels.

That's also when we met Reverend Frederick Douglas Reese. He was born in Selma in 1929. His mother was a teacher, and Reese knew early on that he wanted to become a teacher, too, as well as a preacher. He accomplished both by earning a master's degree in education and a doctorate of divinity.

Reese became pastor of Ebenezer Missionary Baptist Church, and he taught in Selma's segregated school system at R. B. Hudson High School. Determined that African Americans secure their right to vote even in the face of intimidation and police brutality, he led the city's voting rights campaign as president of the Dallas County Voters League and the Selma City Teachers Association.

When a judge prevented Selmians from meeting to talk about civil rights, Reese and members of the voters league met in secret. They became known as the "Courageous Eight."

Six weeks after leading the Teachers' March, Reverend Reese marched on Bloody Sunday, when protesters were beaten by police officers for peacefully demanding their voting rights. Two weeks later, he joined arms with Dr. King as they led hundreds of marchers from Selma to the state capitol in Montgomery for the same cause. For his activism, Reese had smoke bombs hurled at his house and was fired from his job. Undaunted, he became the principal of Selma High School when it was integrated in 1971, and served as assistant superintendent of city schools.

In 1972, Reese became the first African American elected to the Selma city council since Reconstruction.

Wearing his iconic trench coat and a pinstripe suit nearly fifty years after the Teachers' March, Reverend Reese spoke about the importance of the vote. "I tell young people today that they cannot rest on our victories," he said. "That means registering to vote and participating in what this country has to offer."

Reverend Reese died in 2018.

US Army veteran Lawrence Huggins taught physical education and coached at the high school he graduated from: R. B. Hudson High. Huggins said that he and his wife, Dorothea, also a teacher, didn't need convincing to join the Teachers' March because they were "just too enthusiastic to be participating in it."

Coach Huggins was teargassed on Bloody Sunday and marched in the Selma-to-Montgomery march with his students, where he brought along an 8-millimeter camera and recorded the only known color footage of Dr. King preparing for the march. Coach Huggins said that the Teachers' March gave people the courage to get involved in other marches.

"We had a hundred and five new leaders out there," Coach Huggins told us. "They gave the marches the impetus they needed to continue to the next level."

Growing up in Selma, Joyce Parrish O'Neal never missed a mass meeting at Brown Chapel. She was fifteen years old the day her mother, Lula Parrish ("Too Sweet"), participated in the Teachers' March. Mrs. O'Neal remembers the sense of pride she felt when she heard that her mother would be marching, but then fear quickly set in as she realized the danger her mother faced.

Mrs. Parrish enjoyed teaching eighth-grade social studies at Selma's Clark Elementary School. But her frustration grew every time she was told she'd failed the literacy test. "We're college-educated adults and we can't vote and are being denied the vote," she told her daughters. After the Voting Rights Act passed on August 6, 1965, Mrs. Parrish became one of the first African Americans in Selma to register to vote. "She came home with tears of joy," Mrs. O'Neal remembered.

Mrs. O'Neal became director of the Food Assistance Program for the state of Alabama and ran the Alzheimer's Patient Support Group at Brown Chapel, where she conducts tours of the civil rights movement's famous church.

In 2016, Reverend Reese, Coach Huggins, and Mrs. O'Neal were awarded Congressional Gold Medals, as were other Selma foot soldiers of the 1965 civil rights movement.

We will donate a portion of our author proceeds from this book to Brown Chapel and to the R. B. Hudson STEAM Academy in Selma.

ILLUSTRATOR'S NOTE

I am a student of the civil rights movement and keep files of images highlighting this important time in our nation's history. After researching this particular incident and carefully studying provided materials, I hired a photographer to restage multiple images to use as my source material. This allowed me to explore and experiment with spontaneity and fluidity. The result is a body of work that is less controlled and more abstract and primal. The fusion of artistic styles culminated in the perfect stylistic voice.

Coach Lawrence Huggins

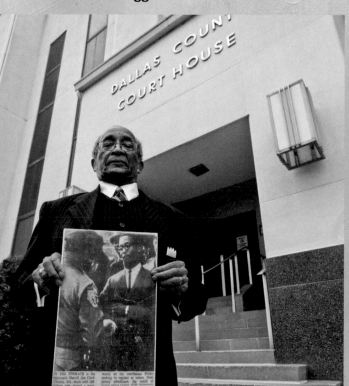

Sheriff Jim Clark consistently blocked the marchers.

TIMELINE

The 1965 Voting Rights Movement in Selma, Alabama (with other key dates)

1936—Founding of Dallas County Voters League (DCVL).

1963—Student Nonviolent Coordinating Committee (SNCC) begins voting-rights efforts in Selma, led by John Lewis.

1964—As a member of the Dallas County Voters League, Reverend F. D. Reese leads voting-rights marches.

July 9, 1964—A judge forbids public discussions, meetings, and marches about voting rights in Selma.

January 1, 1965—A smoke bomb explodes near Selma's Brown Chapel as a warning to voting-rights activists.

January 2, 1965—Dr. Martin Luther King Jr. preaches to 700 people at Brown Chapel in defiance of the judge's order.

January 22, 1965—Reverend F. D. Reese leads the Teachers' March to Selma's Dallas County Courthouse.

February 1, 1965—Dr. Martin Luther King Jr. is arrested and writes his famous "A Letter from a Selma, Alabama, Jail," which is published in the *New York Times* on February 5.

February 10, 1965—Selma students march to courthouse. They are beaten and forced to run several miles.

February 18, 1965—Church deacon Jimmie Lee Jackson is shot near Selma after a peaceful protest. He dies a few days later.

March 7, 1965—Marchers led by John Lewis are beaten by troopers on Selma's Edmund Pettus Bridge.

March 8, 1965—Activists from throughout the US arrive in Selma.

March 9, 1965—Dr. Martin Luther King Jr. leads "Turnaround Tuesday" march across Pettus Bridge.

March 9, 1965—Reverend James Reeb is beaten in Selma. He dies two days later.

March 21–25, 1965—Dr. Martin Luther King Jr. leads 54-mile march from Selma to Montgomery. Reverend Reese and Lawrence Huggins are among the marchers.

March 25, 1965—Activist Viola Liuzzo is killed while transporting marchers back to Selma.

Spring/summer 1965—Protests, arrests, and jailings occur throughout Selma and the South as the voting rights movement continues.

August 6, 1965—President Lyndon B. Johnson signs the Voting Rights Act of 1965. Selma teachers soon register to vote.

August 20, 1965—Voting rights activist Jonathan Myrick Daniels is murdered in Hayneville, AL, a few miles from Selma.

February 24, 2016—Reverend F. D. Reese, Joyce Parrish O'Neal, Lawrence Huggins, and other Selma foot soldiers are awarded Congressional Gold Medals, the highest civilian honor.

April 5, 2018—Reverend F. D. Reese dies at age 88.

Dr. Martin Luther King Jr. and Reverend F. D. Reese join hands with Coretta Scott King as they lead the 1965 voting rights march from Selma to Montgomery.

SELECTED BIBLIOGRAPHY

All quotes used in the book can be found in sources listed with asterisks. *

INTERVIEWS

Conducted by Sandra Neil Wallace and Rich Wallace, in Selma, Alabama

Charles Mauldin, March 2015

Elmyra Martin Smith, March 2015

*Joyce Parrish O'Neal, December 2014 and March 2016

*Lawrence Huggins, March 2016

*Reverend Frederick Douglas Reese, March 2016; and phone interview, June 2016

BOOKS

Branch, Taylor. *At Canaan's Edge: America in the King Years, 1965–68.* New York: Simon & Schuster, 2006.

Fager, Charles E. *Selma 1965: The March That Changed the South.* Boston: Beacon Press, 1985.

Hampton, Henry, and Steve Fayer, with Sarah Flynn. *Voices of Freedom: An Oral History of the Civil Rights Movement from the 1950s through the 1980s.* New York: Bantam Books, 1990.

Lewis, John, with Michael D'Orso. *Walking with the Wind: A Memoir of the Movement.* New York: Harcourt Brace, 1998.

Martin, Jean T. *Civil War to Civil Rights: A Pictorial History of Selma, Alabama.* Portland, OR: Pediment Publishing, 1998.

*Vaughn, Wally G., and Mattie Campbell Davis, eds. *The Selma Campaign, 1963–1965: The Decisive Battle of the Civil Rights Movement.* Dover, MA: Majority Press, 2006.

*Webb, Sheyann, and Rachel West Nelson, as told to Frank Sikora. *Selma, Lord Selma: Girlhood Memories of the Civil-Rights Days.* Tuscaloosa, AL: University of Alabama Press, 1980.

Williams, Juan. *Eyes on the Prize: America's Civil Rights Years, 1954–1965.* New York: Viking, 1987.

FILM AND AUDIO

Birmingham Public Library, *Andrew M. Manis Oral History Interviews Collection.* Tape-recorded interview with Reverend F. D. Reese, by Andrew M. Manis, August, 1, 1989.

Eyes on the Prize: America's Civil Rights Years. Executive producer Henry Hampton, written by Steve Fayer. Blackside, Inc., 1986. PBS.

Selma: The Bridge to the Ballot. Teaching Tolerance, Southern Poverty Law Center. Bill Brummel Productions, 2015.

MAGAZINES, NEWSPAPERS, and JOURNAL ARTICLES

Adelle M. Banks, "Minister Accepts Congressional Medal for Civil Rights Marchers," *Washington Post,* February 25, 2016.

Alvin Benn, "Teachers March Became Example of Civil Disobedience," *Montgomery Advertiser,* March 1, 2015.

Ari Berman, "Fifty Years After Bloody Sunday in Selma, Everything and Nothing Has Changed," *Nation,* February 25, 2015.

Christina Matthews, "Selma: What Has Changed?" *Southern Changes: Journal of the Southern Regional Council, 1978–2003* 13, no. 4 (1991): 12–15. southernchanges.digitalscholarship.emory.edu/sc13-4_1204/sc13-4_005/

"Fifty Arrested at Courthouse Under Charges Named Later," *Selma Times-Journal,* January 19, 1965.

John Herbers, "67 Negroes Jailed in Alabama Drive," *New York Times,* January 20, 1965.

_____. "Alabama Vote Drive Opened by Dr. King," *New York Times,* January 3, 1965.

_____. "Dr. King Punched and Kicked in an Alabama Hotel," *New York Times,* January 19, 1965.

*_____. "Negro Teachers Protest in Selma," *New York Times,* January 23, 1965.

_____."Selma Campaign: A Plea to Nation," *New York Times*, January 22, 1965.

"King Calls for Drive in County on Registration," *Selma Times-Journal*, January 3, 1965.

Martin Luther King, Jr., "A Letter from a Selma, Alabama, Jail," *New York Times*, February 5, 1965.

"Participants in 'Forgotten' Teachers' March Recreate History," *Selma Times-Journal*, January 22, 2015.

Stuart Miller, "Reliving Selma's 'Bloody Sunday,'" *Newsweek*, February 22, 2015.

*Todd Johnson, "Rev. Frederick D. Reese Remembers 'Bloody Sunday' in Selma," *Grio*, March 8, 2010.
thegrio.com/2010/03/08/rev-frederick-d-reese-remembers-bloody-sunday-in-selma

IN-PERSON VISITS (Selma, Alabama)

Brown Chapel AME Church

Clark Elementary School

Dallas County Court House

Ebenezer Missionary Baptist Church

National Voting Rights Museum

Old Depot Museum

Selma 51st Bridge Crossing Jubilee; Foot Soldiers Breakfast, R. B. Hudson Middle School, March 2016

Selma Public Library

LEARN MORE ABOUT THE TEACHERS' MARCH

Hear Reverend F. D. Reese and R. B. Hudson High School teacher/coach Lawrence Huggins discuss the Teachers' March. montgomeryadvertiser.com/story/news/local/selma50/2015/03/01/selma-rev-fd-reese-set-civil-rights-example-early/24214147

Listen to Lawrence Huggins talk about the Teachers' March with radio host Maggie Linton. maggielinton.com/footsoldiers

Teaching Tolerance (Southern Poverty Law Center) includes the Teachers' March in this teaching toolkit and video: *Selma: The Bridge to the Ballot*. tolerance.org/selma-bridge-to-ballot

Watch footage of Dallas County Sheriff Jim Clark arresting civil rights leader Amelia Boynton (3:28); and Reverend Reese and the teachers confronting Clark (3:45). youtube.com/watch?v=smx-Sk3Pzzl

Watch Reverend F. D. Reese receive the Congressional Gold Medal in 2016 on Capitol Hill. speaker.gov/general/speaker-ryan-congressional-leaders-honor-foot-soldiers-1965-voting-rights-marches

Websites active at time of publication

PICTURE CREDITS

To the memory of Reverend F. D. Reese and to the 104 teachers
who marched with him to change voting rights forever.
    —SNW and RW

I dedicate this book to those who were courageous enough to stand up
to the system that refused to give all Americans the right to vote.
Also to the young ones in my family. You all inspire me.
    —CP

ACKNOWLEDGMENTS

Our first thank you goes to Joyce Parrish O'Neal, who told us about the Teachers' March when we first interviewed her
at Brown Chapel about Bloody Sunday. We're grateful to Joyce for revealing her personal story of the march and the
courage of her mother, teacher Lula Parrish. We're also honored to have been two of the last journalists to interview
Reverend F. D. Reese about the Teachers' March. Reverend Reese answered our many questions with such enthusiasm
and invited us to attend Ebenezer Missionary Baptist Church during the week we interviewed him in Selma. To
Lawrence Huggins for sharing his laser-sharp memories of the Teachers' March and welcoming us into his home, where
he showed us his meticulous scrapbook documenting Selma's 1965 voting rights campaign. Finally, to the Selma Public
Library for having microfilm news reports on the Teachers' March ready for us to use in our research, and Lecia Brooks
of the Southern Poverty Law Center for letting us watch footage recorded of the march as seen in their Teaching
Tolerance documentary *Selma: The Bridge to the Ballot.*

Calkins Creek
An imprint of Boyds Mills & Kane,
a division of Astra Publishing House
calkinscreekbooks.com

Printed in the United States of America

ISBN: 978-1-62979-452-5
Library of Congress Control Number:
2019953741

First edition
10 9 8 7 6 5 4 3 2 1

Design by Barbara Grzeslo
The text is set in Gill Sans.
The artwork is acrylic on board.